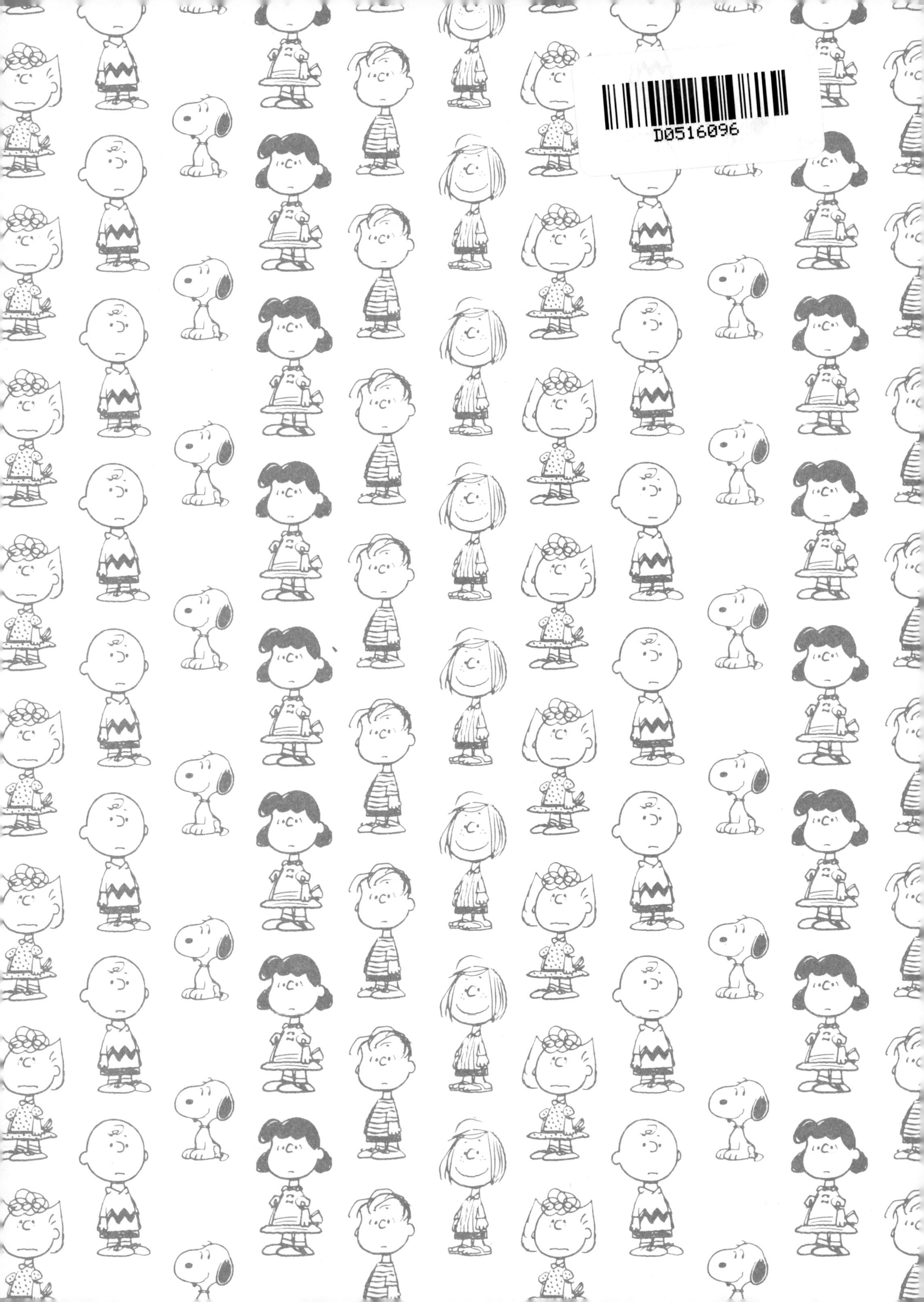

CHARLIE BROWN'S CYCLOPEDIA

PEOPLE AND PLACES
All Around the World

VOLUME · 12 ·

Based on the Charles M. Schulz Characters
Funk & Wagnalls

Photo and Illustration Credits:
Craig Aurness/West Light, 43; Australian Overseas Information Service, 19; Kees Van Den Berg/Photo Researchers, 34; Alouise Boker/Photo Researchers, 39; Jim Brandenburg/West Light, 57; J. Carnemolla/West Light, 19; Al Clayton, Stills Inc./West Light, 49, 52; Louis Gervais/West Light, 16; Rick Golt/Photo Researchers, 45; Don Goode/Photo Researchers, 51; Breck P. Kent/Earth Scenes, 15; R. Kolar/Animals Animals, 23; Larry Lee/West Light, 33; R. Ian Lloyd/West Light, 58; E.A. O'Connell/Earth Scenes, 30; Chuck O'Rear/West Light, 26, 27; Fritz Prenzel/Animals Animals, 14; R. Ingo Riepl/Earth Scenes, 41; D. Roff/West Light, 19; Mary Ellen Senor, 12, 13, 15, 19, 21, 32, 38, 41, 47, 55; Dr. Nigel Smith/Earth Scenes, 48, 50; Brian Vikander/West Light, 22, 24, 28, 42, 56; Mike Yamashita/West Light, 36.

ISBN: 0-8374-0057-0

Part of the material in this volume was previously published in *Charlie Brown's Second Super Book of Questions and Answers.*

Funk & Wagnalls, founded in 1876, is the publisher of *Funk & Wagnalls New Encyclopedia,* one of the most widely owned home and school reference sets, and many other adult and juvenile educational publications.

INTRODUCTION

Welcome to volume 12 of *Charlie Brown's 'Cyclopedia!* Have you ever wondered how the Eskimos keep warm, or who lives on the largest island in the world? Charlie Brown and the rest of the *Peanuts* gang are here to help you find the answers to these questions and many more about people in some faraway places.

Charlie Brown's 'Cyclopedia
has been produced
by Mega-Books of New York,
Inc. in conjunction
with the editorial, design,
and marketing staff of
Field Publications.

**STAFF FOR
MEGA-BOOKS**

Pat Fortunato
Editorial Director

Diana Papasergiou
Production Director

Susan Lurie
Executive Editor

Rosalind Noonan
Senior Editor

Adam Schmetterer
Research Director

**Michaelis/Carpelis
Design Assoc., Inc.**
Art Direction and Design

**STAFF FOR
FIELD PUBLICATIONS**

Cathryn Clark Girard
Assistant Vice President,
Juvenile Publishing

Elizabeth Isele
Executive Editor

Kristina Jorgensen
Executive Art Director

Leslie Erskine
Marketing Manager

Elizabeth Zuraw
Senior Editor

Michele Italiano-Perla
Group Art Director

Kathleen Hughes
Senior Art Director

CONTENTS

When early explorers took to the seas, they made an amazing discovery. The Earth wasn't flat, as they all had thought. It was round! Since then, the Earth has been mapped out by sailors, pilots, and astronauts. Climb aboard Linus's magic blanket, and you, too, can travel around the world with the *Peanut's* gang!

WELCOME TO YOUR WORLD

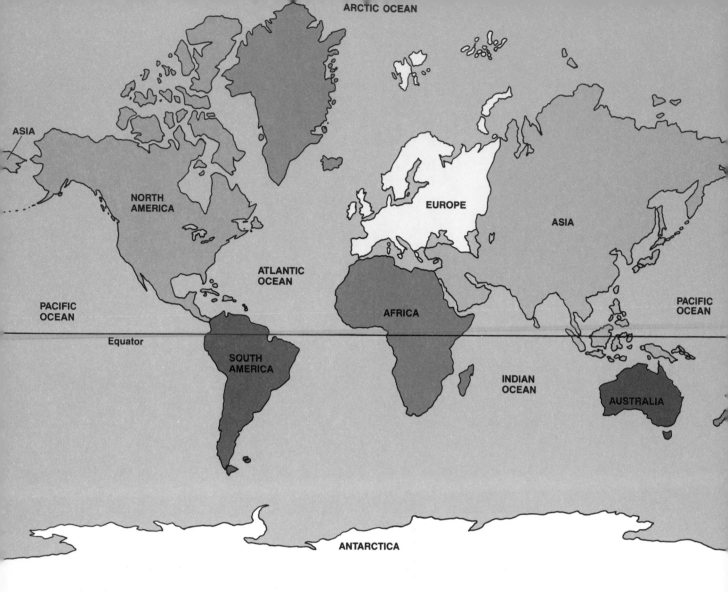

CHAPTER 1

MAPPING OUT THE CONTINENTS

Which continent do you live on?

Look at the map above. Can you find the continent you live on? If you live in the United States, you are on the continent of North America.
If you live in Japan, you are in Asia. If England is your home, your continent is Europe.

What is a continent?

A continent is a large mass of land. Earth has seven continents: Africa, Antarctica, Asia, Australia, Europe, North America, and South America.

What is a map used for?

A map is a drawing that shows an area, usually on the surface of the Earth. Maps tell us about the size and location of land, bodies of water, mountains, and deserts. Maps help travelers find their way. Bodies of water usually appear as blue areas. Can you find the ocean on this map?

THE EQUATOR AND ANTARCTICA

Why is there a line across the center of the map?

The line across the center of the map is the equator. This line divides the world in half. The part of the world above the line is called the Northern Hemisphere. The part under the line is called the Southern Hemisphere. If you traveled to the equator, you would not see an actual line, but you would encounter very hot weather. The equator is the warmest part of the Earth because it receives the Sun's rays most directly.

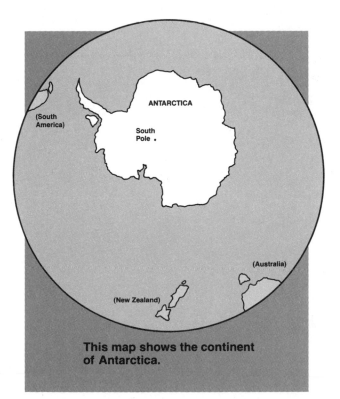

This map shows the continent of Antarctica.

What is the coldest continent?

Antarctica, which some people call the South Pole, is the coldest continent. It is almost completely covered with ice. In some places, the ice is two miles thick. Ninety-five percent of the ice in the world can be found in Antarctica. One Antarctic iceberg was thought to be the size of Belgium, a small country in Europe!

It is so cold in Antarctica that no tree or bush can grow. Scientists visit Antarctica to study it, but they don't stay very long. The only animals there are penguins, birds, and seals. They eat food from the sea.

CHAPTER 2

AUSTRALIA

Our next stop is the world's smallest continent—Australia. It is also the Earth's largest island. This continent has just one country, and that country has the same name as the continent—Australia. Grab your bag, and follow Charlie Brown to the land down under, mate!

DOWN UNDER

THE OUTBACK WILDERNESS

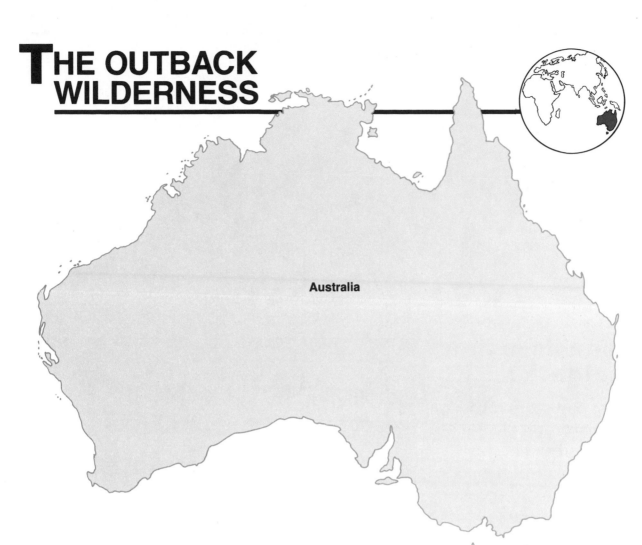

Australia

Why is Australia called the land down under?

Except for Antarctica, Australia is the only continent that is totally south of the equator. Because most of Australia's settlers came from north of the equator, they called it "the land down under."

What is the continent of Australia like?

Most of the people in Australia live in cities around the edge of the island. These cities were built near the water because seaports make cities easy to reach by boat. The land in Australia that doesn't border the ocean is called the outback.

Ayers Rock, found in the Australian outback, is the largest rock in the world.

What is in the outback?

The outback is made up of plains and plateaus—flat land without any trees. Some of the people who live in the outback are sheep or cattle ranchers. Outback ranches are so big that people are very far away from their nearest neighbor. They don't even have telephones! People use two-way radios to talk to their friends.

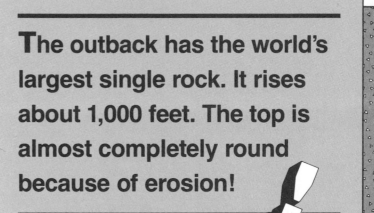

The outback has the world's largest single rock. It rises about 1,000 feet. The top is almost completely round because of erosion!

IF WE WENT TO SCHOOL IN AUSTRALIA, WE WOULDN'T HAVE TO WAIT FOR A STUPID SCHOOL BUS!

How do children go to school in the outback?

Outback children don't "go" to school. They learn their lessons right in their own homes. Their teachers talk to them over the same radio that the people use for talking to neighbors. This school is called School of the Air. Its students must mail their homework and tests to their teachers.

THE BIG CITIES

What do Australian cities look like?

Australian cities look like other big cities in the world. They have some tall office buildings, crowded city streets, and lots of people. Australian cities are a little different, though. They usually are very spread out, with houses instead of apartment buildings. Most Australians like to own their own homes.

What are the city schools like?

They are similar to schools in the United States. Students must go to school from age 6 to 16. Australia also has colleges and universities.

What do city dwellers in Australia do for fun?

Sports are very important to Australians. There are many young people in Australia, and young people usually like to play sports. The weather is warm much of the year, so most sports can be played year round.

Because most of the cities are near water, water sports are very popular. Australians like to swim, sail, fish, and water-ski. Tennis and golf are also popular. Many British games, such as cricket, also are played. Cricket is similar to baseball, but players use a stick called a wicket to hit the ball.

What language do Australians speak?

English is the official language of Australia because the land was settled by people from England. The Australian accent is closer to an English accent than it is to an American accent, but it is still different. Australians also have some different words. Sometimes it is hard for Americans and British people to understand what Australians are talking about even though the Australians are speaking English!

Australian Word	Meaning
jumbuck	sheep
shivoo	party
mate	friend
plonk	wine
willy-willy	windstorm
drongo	fool

C'MON, MATE! WE'VE BEEN INVITED TO A SHIVOO AT CHUCK'S.

PRISONERS AND ABORIGINES

Why did the English settlers move to Australia?

In the 1700s, the jails in England were very crowded. The British people didn't know what to do with all the prisoners. Many of them were in jail just because they disagreed with the king. They weren't dangerous. The English government decided to clean out the jails by sending some of these prisoners to live in Australia.

Were people already living in Australia when the settlers arrived?

Yes, there were people called aborigines. Their life-style was different from that of the new settlers. Many of the aborigines were nomads, people who move from place to place. Although the aborigines had home bases to which they always returned, they were often on the move.

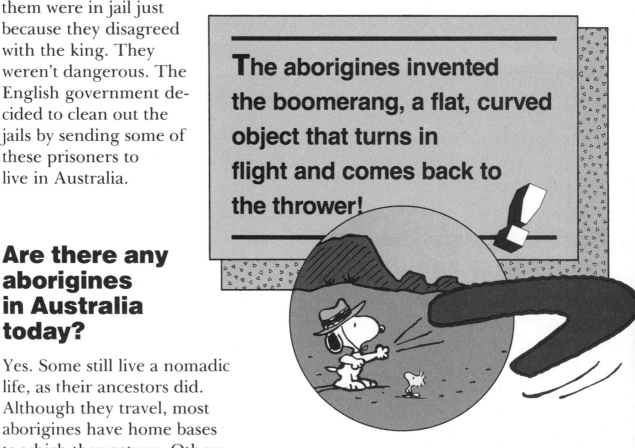

The aborigines invented the boomerang, a flat, curved object that turns in flight and comes back to the thrower!

Are there any aborigines in Australia today?

Yes. Some still live a nomadic life, as their ancestors did. Although they travel, most aborigines have home bases to which they return. Others moved to reservations similar to those in the United States. Many aborigines have moved to the big cities to live side by side with other Australians.

Who else moved to Australia besides the prisoners?

In the mid-1800s, gold was discovered in Australia. Many people came from all over the world, wanting to get rich. Most of these settlers came from England, but some also came from the Americas and China.

Even now, Australians want people to move to their continent. The country has large amounts of empty land available for new settlers. In the past 40 years, two million people have moved to Australia. They are called "new" people.

One out of every six people in Australia is a "new" person!

This aboriginal man is playing a didjeridu (did-you-ree-DEW), a musical instrument that is similar to a flute.

A woman strips the leaves of a palm tree for weaving.

A spear is made with the help of an open fire.

19

CHAPTER 3

THE SECRETS OF ASIA

If you head north from Australia, you'll be in Asia, the world's largest continent. You will see snowy mountains and rice-growing lowlands, skyscrapers in big cities and deserts in remote places, beautiful green islands and for-ever-icy plains. And you'll see millions of fascinating people along the way. All aboard for Asia!

MOUNT EVEREST

THE COUNTRIES OF ASIA

Which countries are on the continent of Asia?

Many countries make up Asia. From the vast lands of the Soviet Union to the tiny islands in the South Pacific, Asia is a land of tremendous variety.

Charlie Brown is going to show you how people live in two fascinating places in Asia, the highest places and the lowest places.

THE HIMALAYAN FAMILIES

What are the Himalayas?

The Himalayas (him-uh-LAY-uhz) are a huge mountain chain in the southern part of Asia. These mountains stretch across three entire countries—Nepal (nuh-PAWL), Sikkim (SICK-im), and Bhutan (boo-TAHN). The Himalayas also touch parts of India, Pakistan, and Tibet. Although the Himalayan people live in different countries, they are alike in many ways.

21

What is the tallest mountain in the world?

Mount Everest, in the Himalayas, is the tallest. It is 5½ miles high! That's almost 20 times as tall as the Empire State Building in New York City. There are 92 peaks in the Himalayas that are more than four miles high.

The highest mountains in the Himalayas get most of their heavy snows in the summer!

Himalayan houses in Nepal

Who lives in the Himalayas?

About 20 million people live there. They have dark, straight hair, dark eyes, and brown skin. Himalayan people are short, but they are strong.

Most people of the Himalayas live in small villages on the narrow strips of land between high mountains. We call these flat, narrow places valleys.

What are Himalayan houses like?

Most are made of stone. Because glass is expensive, there are few windows. The houses also stay warmer without windows. Some houses have flat roofs. Others have roofs with a slight slant. Himalayan people lay heavy stones on top of both kinds of roofs. The stones keep the roofs from blowing off in the strong mountain winds that blow all the time.

Himalayan houses are small, but they have two or three floors. The third floor is used to store food and hay. More food and wood are stored on the ground floor, which also becomes a barn for animals in the winter. The second floor of the house has one big room where the family lives.

In cold weather, the family gathers around an open fire. The fire keeps them warm and cooks their food.

TIBETAN YAK

I THOUGHT WE DOGS WERE MAN'S BEST FRIEND.

Which animal is the best friend of the Himalayan people?

The yak, a big animal that looks like a buffalo, is their best friend. Because yaks can live in rugged mountain areas, they are used for many purposes.

Yaks supply people with meat and milk. They also pull plows for Himalayan farmers, carry heavy loads, and can be ridden like horses. Mountain women weave the yaks' long hair into cloth for blankets and clothing. Yak hide makes warm, sturdy boots.

Even the yaks' horns are useful. They are made into musical instruments.

While looking for grass to eat, yaks have climbed close to the top of Mount Everest!

How do Himalayan people earn a living?

Some raise sheep, goats, or yaks. A few work as guides for tourists and mountain climbers, but most are farmers. They raise cereal crops such as barley and wheat on the mountain slopes. Himalayan people also grow fruits and vegetables in the valleys near their homes.

23

What do Himalayan people eat?

These mountain people eat the cereal and other crops that they raise. Barley, for example, is roasted, then ground, and made into bread. Boiled or fried potatoes are a favorite food.

Yak meat, a treat to Himalayan people, is eaten fresh, or after it has been dried. However, people don't have it often because they like to keep their yaks alive as long as possible. Yaks are killed for meat only when they are quite old. Yak meat is a nice change from sheep and goat meat, which the people eat more often. Himalayan people drink yak milk, and make cheese and butter from it. They also drink tea to which salt and yak butter are added.

These Himalayan children attend school in the local village.

Do Himalayan children go to school?

Some do, and some don't. Only large villages and towns have schools. The mountains make it impossible for children to travel back and forth from one village to another every day. Children from small villages have to leave home for a while to go to school, but not very many do. For that reason a lot of children never learn to read and write. Instead, they learn to plant crops, weave, cook, and do other practical jobs. Children from large towns learn reading, writing, and arithmetic, and some go on to college in other countries.

Do Himalayan villages have stores?

Most Himalayan villages do not have stores. Families grow or make the things they need.

Once a year, a Himalayan family travels to a market town. There, people from all over the mountain area gather to buy and sell goods. Some markets are held outdoors.

Family members take with them the sweaters, blankets, and other things they have made. At the market, they trade for whatever they need: tea, spices, or metal tools. Because they trade one thing for another, many mountain people do not use money.

What do Himalayan people do if they get sick?

Many Himalayan people believe that illness is caused by evil spirits. When these people are ill, they call in a shaman (SHAH-man), an important person who is believed to be able to heal sick people. The shaman tries to cure sickness by dealing with spirits, and by using natural medicines.

For a long time, scientists didn't believe a shaman could really cure a sick person. Doctors have learned, however, that shamans use many plants that are in our medicines.

Many Himalayan people who live in small isolated villages never visit a modern doctor. As a result, some of them die of diseases a modern doctor could cure.

COULD IT BE... ABOMINABLE SNOWMEN?

What is the abominable snowman?

There have been many reports of a shaggy creature, called the abominable snowman, who supposedly lives in the Himalayas. Nobody knows for sure if it really exists, but it is reported to be half human and half ape. Some people say it has a high-pitched scream, a bad smell, and feet that point backward. The Himalayan people's word for the abominable snowman is *yeti* (YET-ee).

The mysterious *yeti* is said to roam the Himalayas at night, but few people can prove that they have ever seen the creature. Others claim that they have seen *yeti* tracks in the snow, but no one has ever proved that a *yeti* made the tracks.

RICE FARMING IN ASIA'S LOWLANDS

What are the lowlands?

The lowlands are the flat, warm areas of Asia below the mountains and on the coast. In Asia, most of the people live in the lowlands.

Rice fields in the lowlands of Indonesia.

SOMETIMES YOU JUST HAVE TO GET YOUR FEET WET.

Where does rice grow?

Rice, the most commonly eaten food in the world, grows in places that are warm, wet, and, usually, low. More rice is grown in Asia than anywhere else. China, India, Indonesia (in-duh-NEE-zhuh), Bangladesh (BANG-luh-desh), Japan, and Thailand (TIE-land) are the six Asian countries that grow the most rice.

Do many people live in the six main rice-growing countries of Asia?

Yes. Nearly two billion people live there. This is slightly less than half the people in the world! The number of people in these countries is growing very fast. In some areas there, people are already terribly crowded.

How can people find enough land to farm in such crowded places?

Most of Asia's rice growers farm small pieces of land. The land on which rice grows is called a paddy. Some paddies are no bigger than a football field, but there are many of these small paddies. Together they produce a lot of rice. The six main rice-growing countries of Asia produce about 260 million tons of rice a year.

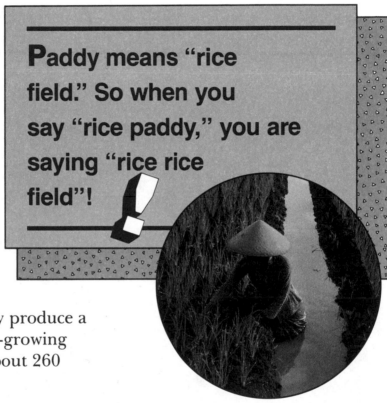

Paddy means "rice field." So when you say "rice paddy," you are saying "rice rice field"!

Which animal helps Asians grow rice?

The water buffalo does. It is a large, strong animal with big horns. In spite of its size, the water buffalo is a gentle animal. A child can safely lead one through the fields.

When a rice farmer plows his paddy, a water buffalo usually pulls the plow. The plow makes ditches in the earth. Then rice seeds are planted in the ditches. From the seeds, stalks grow a few feet high. On the stalks grow the grains that people eat. When the grains are ripe, the stalks are cut down and put on a cart pulled by a water buffalo. The stalks are then spread on the ground. The water buffalo walks over them, forcing the grains off the stalks.

Do rice farmers use any farm machines?

Most paddies are too small for the rice farmer to use farm machines. Instead the work is done by hand. All the family members help to plant the rice and pull weeds from the paddy. When the rice is ripe, they cut it with sharp knives.

Some rice farmers, however, have begun using tractors to pull their plows.

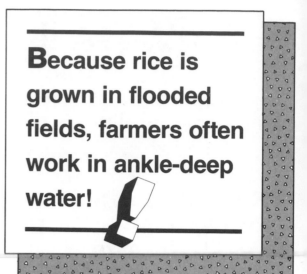

Because rice is grown in flooded fields, farmers often work in ankle-deep water!

Asian rice farmers build their houses on stilts to keep them from being flooded.

Where do rice farmers build their houses?

Rice farmers build their houses in villages. They do not live right next to their fields, as American farmers do. Each morning, the rice farmers walk from the village to their paddies. At the end of the day, they walk back home.

In some rice-growing areas, there are few roads. Rivers and canals go to more places than roads do, so the people usually travel in rowboats and canoes.

Rice farmers who live near a canal use its waters for bathing, cooking, brushing their teeth, and washing their clothes!

IMAGINE...NO READING, WRITING, OR ARITHMETIC! SOME KIDS HAVE ALL THE LUCK!

Are there schools for rice farmers' children?

There are schools only in some places. In China and Japan, there are schools for the children of all rice-farming families. In other countries, only the largest villages have schools. In some places, teachers visit middle-sized villages for a few months at a time. They teach children to read, write, and do arithmetic, but many children who grow up in small, poor villages never learn to read and write.

29

What do rice farmers eat?

Rice! Asian rice farmers usually boil their rice, but they also eat it steamed or fried. Sometimes they cover the rice with a sauce made from boiled fish.

Some rice-growing families also raise and eat sweet potatoes, beans, peas, or other vegetables. A family might have a few fruit trees, some chickens, and a pig. Now and then, they go fishing, or they buy a fish, but the poorest rice farmers have little to eat besides rice.

Some markets are on water. Here, pots are offered for sale.

Where do rice farmers go shopping?

In the nearest town. Few small villages have stores of their own. For some rice-growing families, going shopping means taking a boat ride on a river or a canal. Other families walk a few miles. In some places, they can ride part of the way in a small bus. Families often take along something to sell at the town market.

Do rice farmers' villages have doctors?

Most villages do not have doctors. A family of rice farmers may live their whole lives without ever visiting a doctor, but some are visited by a shaman. Many of Asia's rice farmers believe that they are surrounded by spirits. They think that spirits live in every field and every house. To these rice farmers, illness means that someone has upset the spirits. When someone is sick, the rice farmers do what the Himalayan people do. They call in a shaman, who tells the sick person how to bring back harmony with the spirits.

30

From the vineyards of France to the busy streets of London, England and Madrid, Spain; from the fishing villages of Greece to the art museums of Italy; from mountain chalets in Switzerland to rolling farmlands in Poland and centers of industry in Germany—every country in Europe is special, but one is like no other. It's the Netherlands. So take a ride on Woodstock's windmill to this special place.

WINDMILLS OF EUROPE

THE COUNTRIES OF EUROPE

Norway
United
Kingdom
Finland
Sweden
Denmark
Netherlands
Ireland
Germany
(West and
East)
Poland
Belgium
Luxembourg
Czech and Slovak
Federal Republic
France
Austria
Switzerland
Hungary
Spain
Italy
Yugoslavia
Romania
Bulgaria
Portugal
Albania
Greece
Turkey
Union of
Soviet
Socialist
Republics

What countries are in the continent of Europe?

This map shows you all the countries in Europe. Some European countries such as Monaco are smaller than many cities in the United States, while others are the size of some of our states. You'll find warm weather in the southern regions of Spain and boot-shaped Italy. In northern Finland and Norway, however, there's so much snow, you'll need a sled to get around!

THE NETHERLANDS

Why is the Netherlands unusual?

The Netherlands, often called Holland, has many rivers, but no mountains. Much of this country is situated below sea level. This means that the land is lower than the level of the sea. The word *netherland* means "low land."

Are there any farms in the Netherlands?

Dutch farms are called *polders*. A *polder* is a section of land that was once underwater. Dutch *polders* are used for growing grain, potatoes, beets, and tulips. Dutch farmers also raise cows. More than half of this country is farmland.

Windmills in the Netherlands

How is water kept out of the *polders*?

The Dutch have built many high walls called dikes to hold back the water from the land. Rain and groundwater are removed with pumps, which are at work all the time. These pumps were once run by windmills, but now they are powered by electricity. Although they are not used as much as in the past, windmills still dot the countryside.

Do the dikes ever break?

Most farmers keep a very close watch on the dikes to make sure they don't break. Storks help the farmers, too! These birds eat small animals that dig into the dike walls to make homes.

Dikes hold back the sea and protect the land in the Netherlands.

Are floods a problem?

Yes. Floods bring a lot of water that presses against the dikes. Sandbags and mats made from tree branches are used to make the dikes stronger.

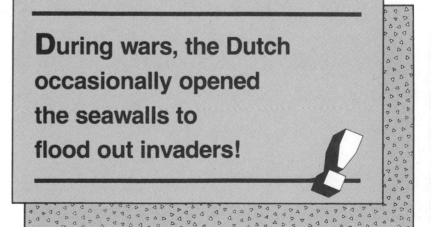
During wars, the Dutch occasionally opened the seawalls to flood out invaders!

34

HOW THE DUTCH LIVE

What do the Dutch people do for a living?

As in many places in Europe, some Dutch people work in the tourist business. A lot of other people work in manufacturing. All the rivers and the sea make the Netherlands a good place for trade. Boats can travel by river into the rest of Europe and out into the ocean very easily. Many Dutch people are expert sailors.

What do Dutch farmhouses look like?

A Dutch farmhouse is a house and a barn all in one. The part people live in looks a lot like an American home. In the barn, there are stalls for the cows, and a room for cheese-making. The Dutch produce a lot of cheese and other milk products.

What do Dutch people wear?

Dutch people wear clothes like those worn in the United States and Europe. Dutch farmers, though, do like to wear wooden shoes. These shoes are good for walking in the wet *polders*. Leather shoes would fall apart quickly.

Wax-covered cheese is sold at an open market in the Netherlands.

Do Dutch people go shopping?

Yes. There are many shops and stores in the Netherlands. When the weather is nice, there are open markets in the main squares of some Dutch towns. Shoppers can buy tulips, vegetables, and delicious, creamy cheeses made in the Netherlands.

How do Dutch people travel through their country?

The many canals and rivers make boat travel easy, but the most popular way to travel is by bicycle. The land is very flat, so biking is easy. Biking is also economical, since gas for cars is expensive.

Do Dutch children go to school?

All Dutch children from 6 to 16 years of age attend school. Students attend a primary school for six years. After that, they may attend different types of secondary schools. Some secondary schools prepare students for college. Many of these students will go on to study medicine or science. Some secondary schools help train students for jobs as carpenters, electricians, or secretaries. There are special secondary schools just to teach teachers.

CHAPTER 5

Some of Africa is covered by desert or tropical jungles, and throughout Africa, there are many big cities. Most of the continent, however, is savannah—open grassland with a few trees. Because of its rough and unfamiliar terrain, travelers in the nineteenth century found it hard to explore Africa. Since no one knew much about this country, it was nicknamed the "dark continent."

THE DARK CONTINENT OF AFRICA

THE COUNTRIES OF AFRICA

Which countries are in the continent of Africa?

Many countries are on the large continent of Africa, and no other continent has as many different groups of people. There are Berbers who live in the mountains and deserts of the north, and Kung Bushman hunters who roam the southwest. Tall Masai warriors live in the eastern lands of Kenya and Tanzania, and the Ashanti, whose beautiful sculpture has inspired many American and European artists, live in the west, on the Guinea Coast. The world's oldest civilization was born on the continent of Africa, along the great Nile River in the country of Egypt. We will visit some of the interesting people who call Africa home.

Tunisia
Morocco
Algeria
Libya
Egypt
Western Sahara
Mauritania
Mali
Niger
Senegal
Gambia
Guinea-Bissau
Burkina Faso
Chad
Sudan
Djibouti
Guinea
Nigeria
Ethiopia
Ivory Coast
Benin
Central African Republic
Uganda
Somalia
Sierra Leone
Liberia
Togo
Ghana
Cameroon
Equatorial Guinea
Congo
Kenya
Gabon
Rwanda
Burundi
Tanzania
Zaire
Angola
Malawi
Mozambique
Zambia
Namibia
Zimbabwe
Botswana
Lesotho
Swaziland
Madagascar
South Africa

AFRICAN PYGMIES

Who lives in the jungles of central Africa?

Many different groups of people, often called tribes, live there. The largest race of people there are called African pygmies. Most pygmies are short—less than five feet tall.

When pygmies have a celebration, such as a wedding, they ask the forest to be happy!

How do pygmies get food?

Most pygmy men are hunters. Women gather fruits and roots. They also fish. Sometimes pygmies trade their meat with nearby farmers in exchange for vegetables.

Pygmies use bows and arrows and spears for hunting. If they are hunting an animal that is very fast and might escape, they put poison on the tips of their arrows and spears. Pygmies also use nets to capture animals before they are killed for food. All of the families make nets, which are tied together. Then the animals are driven into the nets. All animals captured for food are shared by everyone.

Do pygmies always share food?

Yes, they share because pygmies believe in working together. If there is an argument between two people, the tribe gets together to settle it. There is no leader. In general, pygmies are peaceful people.

Pgymy men working in their village.

What do pygmies' houses look like?

To build a house, pygmies bend light, wooden poles together into a dome. The poles are covered with large leaves which also are used to make beds. Smaller leaves are used as dishes and cups.

What are pygmies' clothes like?

Clothing is made from the bark of the bongi tree. The bark is beaten and stretched before it is made into clothing. Because the weather is very hot, pygmies don't wear much at all.

Do pygmy children go to school?

Pygmy children don't attend school. Instead, their parents teach them how to hunt and gather food.

THE PEOPLE OF THE SAHARA

What is the world's largest desert?

The Sahara (suh-HAR-uh), in northern Africa, is the largest desert in the world. It is about the same size as the United States.

Sahara means both "desert" and "wilderness" in Arabic, the language of some of the Saharan people. A wilderness is a land that people have not yet changed or used. The modern Sahara has some towns, highways, factories, mines, and oil fields, but most of it is still a wilderness. Living there is very hard.

Some parts of the Sahara are sandy. Others are rocky, but all parts are hot and sunny during the day and cool at night.

Is all of the Sahara covered with sand?

No. Most of the Sahara Desert does *not* have sand on it! In some areas, tiny pebbles called gravel cover the ground. The middle of the Sahara has the most sand.

A pile of sand formed by the wind is called a sand dune. A few sand dunes in the Sahara are as high as the tallest buildings in the world!

Who lives in the Sahara Desert?

There are three groups of people who live in the Sahara. The Moors live in the west. The Tuareg (TWAH-reg) live in the central part. The Tibbu (TIH-boo) live in the east. Each of these groups speaks a different language and has its own customs. Because they all live in the desert, however, their way of life is similar.

AFRICAN NOMAD

Thousands of years ago, the Sahara wasn't a desert. Old drawings in Saharan caves show people in canoes!

How do desert people get water?

Even a desert has underground water in some places. Such a place is called an oasis (oh-AY-sis). At an oasis, the water may rise to the surface and form a spring or water hole. If it doesn't, people can dig a well to reach the water. In the Sahara, there are 90 big oases.

Before desert people leave an oasis, they fill goatskin bags with water. In this way, they have a supply of water while they travel.

WHY DID I THINK THIS WOULD WORK?

How do desert people get food?

Some people live at an oasis and grow crops for food. They use ditches or pipes to run water from a well or spring to the crops. This system is called irrigation (ihr-ih-GAY-shun). Other desert people travel from one spot in the desert to another. These people are called nomads. They raise herds of animals and buy fruits and vegetables whenever they pass through a town.

Desert people can buy vegetables and grain from shops like this one when they pass through towns.

Why do nomads travel from one spot to another?

Most nomads keep traveling to find food and water for their herds of camels, sheep, or goats. Animals quickly eat the few plants that grow in the desert. Then the nomads have to find a new desert pasture, which is sometimes miles and miles away. When they get to a new pasture, they unpack and set up camp, but soon they will move again.

How do nomads carry all their supplies?

Supplies are carried on the backs of their camels. Camels can carry heavy loads. They are great helpers to desert nomads. Camels' soft, wide feet don't sink deeply into sand, so they can walk easily in the desert. Camels can also go without drinking water for a long time—seven to ten days when traveling. When there is little food, a camel can live on the fat stored in its hump.

Because camels are good at carrying supplies, some desert people use them to make a living. The camels carry supplies across the desert to be sold. People who sell things are called merchants. Desert merchants often travel together in groups called caravans (CARE-uh-vanz). A caravan can protect its members against robbers better than a few people traveling alone.

In the winter, a camel that does not work or travel can go without water for as long as two months!

How else do camels help desert people?

Camels not only *carry* supplies, but they *are* supplies themselves! Nomads drink camel milk and eat camel meat. From camel skins, nomads make leather for tents. From camel hair, they make wool clothes. Camels can also carry tired desert travelers on their backs.

What do nomads' houses look like?

Most nomads live in tents made of camel skins held up with poles. At moving time, the nomads fold up their tents and load them onto camels. Because nomads are moving all the time, they don't use the same kind of furniture that we do. They use mats woven from palm branches. Nomads use the mats for chairs, tables, and beds.

From years of walking on hot sand, the soles of nomads' feet are tough. Some can put their feet in a low fire and not feel it!

Do nomad children go to school?

Some do, but most nomad children do not attend a school like the one you go to. However, the governments of a few Saharan countries send teachers to nomads' camps so that children can get some schooling.

An Arabian family dines on a midday meal of rice.

What do nomads eat?

When desert families have guests, they often serve sheep or lamb that has been roasted over an open fire. On ordinary days, a desert cook boils the meat of a sheep, a lamb, or a chicken. Chick-peas and cut-up vegetables such as carrots, onions, and beans go into the same pot. A desert family also eats a dish called *couscous* (KOOS-koos), a cereal mixed with meat and vegetables.

Camel cheese and camel butter are also popular foods. Camel cheese is made from camel milk. Camel butter isn't. Camel butter is the fat taken from the camel's hump after the animal is killed. People spread it on certain foods, or just dip their fingers in it and eat it plain. Desert people drink sweet tea, goat milk, or camel milk.

45

Now let's sail across the Atlantic Ocean from Africa to South America. South America has modern cities, but much of it is covered by one of the world's great natural wonders— a huge rain forest!

THE WONDERS OF SOUTH AMERICA

THE COUNTRIES OF SOUTH AMERICA

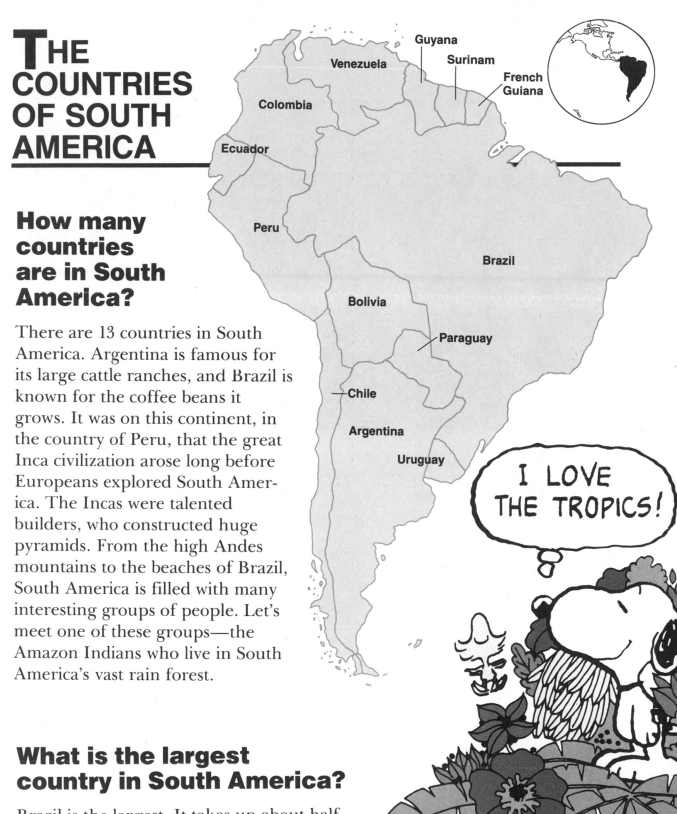

How many countries are in South America?

There are 13 countries in South America. Argentina is famous for its large cattle ranches, and Brazil is known for the coffee beans it grows. It was on this continent, in the country of Peru, that the great Inca civilization arose long before Europeans explored South America. The Incas were talented builders, who constructed huge pyramids. From the high Andes mountains to the beaches of Brazil, South America is filled with many interesting groups of people. Let's meet one of these groups—the Amazon Indians who live in South America's vast rain forest.

What is the largest country in South America?

Brazil is the largest. It takes up about half the continent. Some Brazilians live in modern cities. Others belong to tribes that live in the rain forest.

THE PEOPLE OF THE AMAZON RAIN FOREST

In the morning, a mist hangs over the Amazon's tropical rain forest. The words *tropic* and *tropical* are often used to refer to the hot regions around the equator.

What is a rain forest?

A rain forest is a very warm, very rainy place where many trees grow. Because of the rain, the trees grow tall and close together. The covering of treetops is so thick that it blocks out the wind, making the air below still and uncomfortable. The treetops also keep sunlight from reaching the ground. Because most plants need sunlight to live, few low plants can grow in much of the rain forest. It is quite easy to walk through these shaded areas that have few low plants. A rain forest has many different kinds of animals. These include birds, crocodiles, anteaters, lizards, snakes, and big cats called jaguars. The list also includes thousands of different kinds of insects, some of which are harmful or just bothersome to people.

The largest rain forest in the world is in South America, around the Amazon River. Most of the rain forest is in Brazil, but parts are in eight other countries. This rain forest is 3,000 miles long!

Is the rain forest the same as a jungle?

No. A jungle is a part—the thickest part—of a rain forest. It usually grows in places where people have chopped down the tall trees. After the area has been cleared, many ground plants grow quickly. In fact, plants grow on and over and around each other. This makes a jungle a very hard place to walk through.

How much rain falls in the Amazon rain forest?

A lot! In the wettest places, about 100 inches of rain falls in a year. That is more than twice the rainfall of New York City each year, and six times the yearly rainfall in Los Angeles.

There is always rain falling somewhere in the Amazon rain forest!

In the rain forest, the wettest months are called the rainy season. Then heavy rain falls during part of every day. The rest of the year is the dry season, but even that is not very dry. It's just less wet!

Who lives in the Amazon rain forest?

Groups of people we call Indians live there. These people are distantly related to the Indians of North America, but they look very different. They have darker skin and shorter bodies than North American Indians. Because they live in a rain forest, their way of life is very different, and their languages are different, too.

Until recently, the Amazon Indians lived exactly as their ancestors had lived thousands of years ago. The dense, rain forest kept them separated from the rest of the world, but today, life for the Amazon Indians is changing.

This Amazon father and son are natives of the rain forest.

What kind of houses do Amazon Indians build?

Some Amazon Indians build houses that look like haystacks. The houses are made of dried palm leaves or dried grasses. A frame of thin poles holds the "hay" in place.

Other Amazon Indians use the dried palm leaves only for roofs. They make the walls of their houses from either thin tree trunks or mud.

AMAZON HOUSES

How do these houses look inside?

Each house has one very big room. The floor is a natural dirt floor. The room has some stools made from tree trunks. It has hammocks to sleep in. There are no windows, so the house is dark. Sometimes the Amazon Indians build a fire inside to cook their food, but most of the time, they cook outdoors.

In many Amazon houses, parents, children, grandparents, aunts, and uncles all live together. Sometimes as many as 70 people live in one house!

What do rain forest people eat?

They eat many kinds of fruits and vegetables. They grow some in their gardens and gather some in the forest. They also hunt and fish for food.

Corn and cassava (kuh-SAH-vuh) are the most important crops in the Amazon rain forest. Cassava is the plant from which we make tapioca pudding. The Amazon Indians make cakes from it. They roast corn and make a soup of ground corn. They also raise and eat sweet potatoes.

Trees in the forest supply the native people with fruits and nuts, and bees provide them with honey. Some Amazon Indian groups are always on the lookout for a tree with a beehive in it. When they see one, they chop the tree down, take the honey from the hive, and eat it.

Amazon Indians also eat wild pigs, monkeys, armadillos (are-muh-DILL-oze), turtles, and fish. They roast the meat and fish over an open fire.

50

Amazon waters contain vicious piranha (pih-RAHN-yuh) fish. One piranha can fit in your hand. A group of piranhas could eat you up in just a few minutes!

Do the Amazon Indians hunt with guns?

Yes. Sometimes they use shotguns to hunt large ground animals. For hunting birds, fish, and other small animals, however, they rely on their old ways—spears, blowguns, or bows and arrows.

Amazon Indians are very skilled hunters who can hit fast-moving animals with their arrows and darts. They can even hit fish with their arrows!

Rain forest hunters use bamboo stems to make long arrows and thin strips of palm wood to make bow strings. Some bows are as long as six feet, longer than the height of some hunters!

A blowgun is a long, hollow bamboo pole. Through it, a hunter blows poison darts.

Amazon people use river boats to travel through the rain forest.

Some of the Amazon Indians hunt at night with the help of flashlights!

Is it true that Amazon Indians wear no clothing?

Many Amazon Indians of the rain forest wear little or no clothing. Some wear only belts, arm bands, jewelry, or headbands. Some wear only tiny skirts called loincloths.

For special occasions, these rain forest natives paint their bodies with different colored dyes made from jungle plants. Some of the designs they use stand for animals in the rain forest.

Is it true that Amazon Indians of the rain forest are unfriendly?

Some of them dislike strangers. In the past, explorers hurt and killed many of them, and some were forced to work as slaves by people who came to take rubber from the forest's rubber trees.

Other Amazon Indians are shy rather than un-friendly. They are frightened by visitors, who are very different from themselves. Often, though, these native people learn to accept visitors as friends.

52

Who teaches the rain forest children?

Children are taught mostly by parents, friends, relatives, and older children, but they don't learn reading, writing, and arithmetic. Instead, children learn the skills they will need when they grow up. Girls learn how to cook, plant crops, and search for honey and fruit. They also practice weaving cloth. Boys learn to hunt and fish.

There are a few modern schools in the Amazon rain forest today. They were set up by the government of Brazil. In these schools, children read books and take tests—just as you do.

Do Amazon children have time for toys?

Yes, they do, but they have to make their own. Sometimes their parents help them. They use cornstalks, bits of wood, bones—whatever they can find—to make dolls, toy animals, and balls to play with.

In an Amazon Indian relay race, each man who runs carries a 100-pound log on his shoulders!

THIS ISN'T EASY!

What happens when people get sick in the rain forest?

Many Amazon Indians believe that evil spirits cause illness. When someone gets sick, a shaman is called. The shaman tries to cure the person by dealing with the spirits and by using natural medicines. Jungle villages do not have modern doctors and nurses. However, Brazilian doctors and nurses sometimes visit the rain forest to take care of sick people. There are now some Amazon Indian nurses and medical teams.

CHAPTER 7

From bustling cities to busy farming towns to quiet fishing villages— North America has something for everyone. It also has a place that might be fun to visit, if you don't mind frosty weather. Come follow Snoopy for a snow-crunching trip to the land of the Eskimos (ES-kuh-moze).

NEXT STOP: NORTH AMERICA

THE COUNTRIES OF NORTH AMERICA

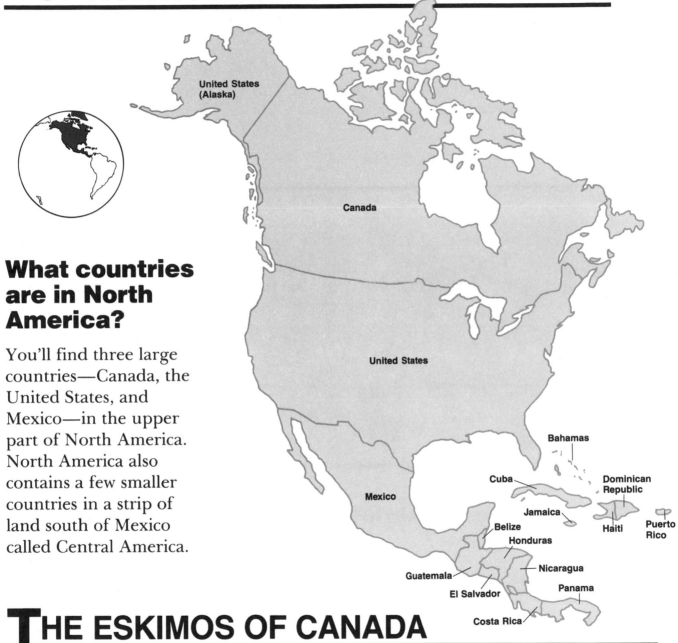

What countries are in North America?

You'll find three large countries—Canada, the United States, and Mexico—in the upper part of North America. North America also contains a few smaller countries in a strip of land south of Mexico called Central America.

Map labels: United States (Alaska), Canada, United States, Mexico, Bahamas, Cuba, Dominican Republic, Jamaica, Haiti, Puerto Rico, Belize, Honduras, Guatemala, Nicaragua, El Salvador, Panama, Costa Rica

THE ESKIMOS OF CANADA

Who lives in the coldest parts of North America?

Eskimos—or Inuits—do. Inuit is the name that most Eskimos call themselves. They live in northern Canada, Alaska, and Greenland. These cold regions near the North Pole are called arctic (ARK-tick) regions. There are only about 50,000 Eskimos in the world.

Do the Eskimos ever have warm weather?

Yes. The northern part of North America gets warm in the summer, but never hot. The average summer temperature there is about 50 degrees Fahrenheit. The summer temperature often drops below freezing, and sometimes it even snows! Although the ground isn't always covered with snow, it is always frozen below the surface. This frozen area is called permafrost.

Only strong plants can grow during the short, cool arctic summer. In spite of this, there are several kinds of arctic plants.

Eskimos wear warm clothing that is often quite colorful.

Do Eskimos live in igloos?

Although most modern Eskimos live in houses, some still live in igloos. These Eskimos move into tents in the summer months. Even though most Eskimos don't live in igloos, they still know how to build them from snow blocks. In igloos, even the beds are made out of snow blocks!

What do the Eskimos wear to keep warm?

Eskimos bundle up in warm clothes that are made out of fur, and they sleep under fur blankets. When it is very cold, Eskimos put on two layers of everything. The first layer of fur goes against their skin. In the second layer, the fur is worn on the outside. Eskimos also wear fur boots called *mukluks* (MUCK-lucks). The outer soles are made from the skin of a moose or seal, and the tops are made from canvas or caribou (KAR-uh-boo) skin. A caribou is a kind of deer that lives in the arctic.

Teams of dogs pull Eskimo sleds across the snow.

How do Eskimos travel over the snow?

At one time, Eskimos traveled in sleds pulled by dogs. Some Eskimos still travel this way, but most now use snowmobiles. For long distances, they use airplanes that have skis on them to help the planes land on ice.

For travel on water, Eskimos use motorboats, kayaks, and umiaks (OO-me-aks). Kayaks and umiaks are made of animal skins stretched over a wooden frame.

What games do Eskimos play?

Eskimos do a lot of playing indoors where it is warm. One of the games they play is like darts. The Eskimos make holes in a pair of antlers, hang them from the ceiling, and then try to throw sticks through the holes.

In spite of the cold weather, Eskimos still do play outdoors. Naturally, they play in the snow or on ice. Eskimo children like to speed downhill on sleds. They also enjoy other cold weather sports such as ice hockey and ice skating.

Are there schools for Eskimo children?

There are schools, but only in large villages. Children who live in small villages must leave their families to get an education. When they are ready to start first grade, they move to a village that has a school. Children from a few villages live together in a large building. Usually there are fewer than 30 children. At the end of the school year, the children go home.

DID YOU KNOW...?

SIBERIA, HERE I COME!

GREAT WALL OF CHINA

- The Soviet Union is on two continents—Asia and Europe. Most of the country is in a part of Asia called Siberia, but not many people live in this cold, snowy part. The rest of the country is in Europe, where most of the Soviet Union's cities are. Greece and Turkey are also on two continents.

- The Great Wall of China lives up to its name! This amazing wall is 2,150 miles long, with many more miles of branches. In some sections, the wall rises to 39 feet above the ground! Built of earth and stone, it is 32 feet thick. The Great Wall was built by a Chinese emperor. He wanted to stop Mongolian horsemen from invading his country, but the plan didn't work. The invaders broke through the wall.

THAT'S A GREAT WALL YOU'RE BUILDING, LINUS!

• Have you ever traded marbles or baseball cards? If you have, you've used a system called bartering. All sorts of things have been bartered in the past—beads, shells, animal skins, feathers, and food. Today, most countries use money printed by their governments. Money has pictures and symbols that have meaning for the people who live in that country. Some people still don't use money. They barter for things they need. They might barter—trade—a chicken for a piece of cloth or a bushel of apples or an ax.

• Mexico City is sinking! The capital city of Mexico was built on a plateau on top of water. This water is pumped out of the soil and used for drinking water. As the water level in the soil gets lower, the soil gets lower, too. This means that the streets and buildings on top of the soil sink. Since 1900, parts of Mexico City have sunk as much as 25 feet!

• Most Eskimo dogs, called huskies, stay outside all the time, even in the coldest weather. They have very thick fur. To keep warm while they sleep, they spin around and around until they have made a hole in the snow. Then they snuggle down into the hole, which protects them from the wind.

I'D RATHER USE A NICE BLANKET TO KEEP WARM!

◆ IN THE ◆
NEXT VOLUME

Have you ever wondered how a light bulb works, or why batteries go dead, or how a picture appears on your television? You'll find the answers to these questions and lots more in volume 13, *Electricity and Magnetism—Invisible Forces.*

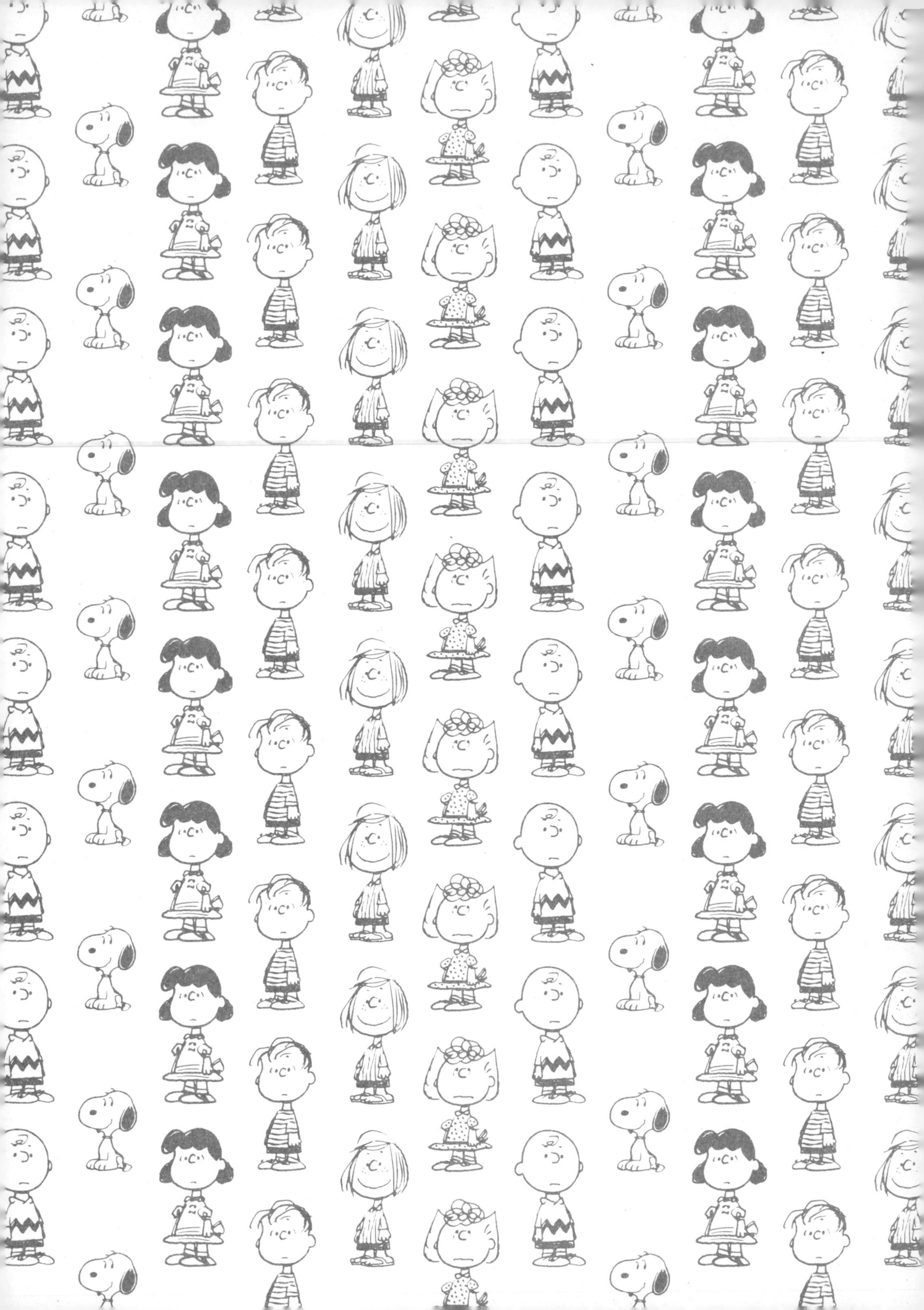